WITHDRAWN

P9-EKC-854

FOOD & FEASTS

IN THE

Middle Ages

Imogen Dawson

New York

First American publication 1994 by New Discovery Books,
A Division of Simon & Schuster
299 Jefferson Road, Parsippany, NJ 07054

First published in 1994 in Great Britain by
Wayland (Publishers) Ltd

A ZOË BOOK

Copyright © 1994 Zoë Books Limited

Devised and produced by
Zoë Books Limited
15 Worthy Lane
Winchester
Hampshire SO23 7AB
England

All rights reserved. No part of this book may be reproduced
or transmitted in any form or by any means, electronic or
mechanical, including photocopying, recording, or by any
information storage and retrieval system, without
permission in writing from the Publisher.

Printed in Belgium by Proost N.V.
Design: Jan Sterling, Sterling Associates
Picture research: Victoria Sturgess
Maps: Gecko Limited
Production: Grahame Griffiths

10 9 8 7 6 5 4 3 2

Library of Congress Cataloging–in–Publication Data

Dawson, Imogen.
    Food & feasts in the Middle Ages / Imogen Dawson.
        p. cm. — (Food & feasts)
    Includes bibliographical references and index.
    ISBN 0-02-726324-X (LSB) ISBN 0-382-39571-9 (pbk)
    1. Food habits—Europe—History—Juvenile literature.
    2. Civilization, Medieval—Juvenile literature. [1. Food
    habits—Europe—History. 2. Civilization, Medieval.]
    I. Title. II. Series.
    GT2853.E8F66 1994
    394.1'2'094—dc20   93-27200

Summary: A social history of the Medieval period,
explaining why certain foods were eaten and how they
were eaten, and what events brought about special
celebrations and feasts.

Photographic acknowledgments

The publishers wish to acknowledge, with thanks, the
following photographic sources:

Ancient Art & Architecture Collection 5t & c, 8t, 9tl, 10c
& b, 11c, 14tl, 19t; The Bodleian Library, Oxford 3
(Ms.Rawl.G.98, fol.49v), 4b (Ms.Douce 374, fol.17r), 7b
(Ms.Canon.Liturg.99, fol.16r),11b (Ms.Douce 5, fol.7r),
13t ,23t (Ms.Bodl.264, fol. 218r), 25b (Ms.Bodl.264,
fol. 239r); The Bridgeman Art Library / Musée Conde,
Chantilly title page, 9tr, 19b / British Library,London
16b, 17t, 18t; The British Library,London 12tl & b,23b;
Mary Evans Picture Library 4t, 18b, 20t & b; The Fotomas
Index 13b; Sonia Halliday Photographs 6t, 7t, 14b; Robert
Harding Picture Library 13c, 17b; Hulton Deutsch
Collection 8b, 11t, 21; Mansell Collection 6b, 14tr, 16t,
24b; Bild-Archiv der Österreichischen Nationalbibliothek,
Wien 15t; Stadtbibliothek, Nürnberg 15c; The Board of
the Trustees of the Victoria & Albert Museum 10t.

Cover: Ancient Art & Architecture Collection center;
Sonia Halliday Photographs bottom right; Robert Harding
Picture Library bottom left; Hulton Deutsch Collection
top left
Cover illustration top right: Cecilia Fitzsimons

The publishers have made every effort to trace the
copyright holders, but if they have inadvertently
overlooked any, they will be pleased to make the
necessary arrangement at the first opportunity.

Contents

Introduction

▽ *Trenchers*, thick slices of stale brown bread with a slight hollow in the middle, were used as plates. Rich people ate round bread called *manchets*, which were placed next to the stack of trenchers at the beginning of the feast.

The diners helped themselves to the dishes that were served. They used spoons, knives, and—most commonly—their fingers.

◁ Roast meat and fish are being served on **spits** at this 11th-century banquet or feast. The diners are using only their knives. Forks were not generally used at the table, except in Greece and Italy, where they were used to eat **sweetmeats**.

The period of history in Europe that we call the Middle Ages lasted for more than 1,000 years—from the end of the Roman Empire until about A.D. 1500. During this time most people in Europe became Christian. As the Church became more powerful, the **monasteries** held lands in every state and kingdom in Europe.

The rules of the Church included the foods that could be eaten on each day of the week and at different times of the year. These rules were important in the everyday lives of both rich and poor people.

Most people lived in the countryside, working the land under the **feudal system**. Lords and knights were given land, or **manors**, by the ruler. In return they promised that they and their men would fight for that ruler. These nobles controlled the land from their castles and houses.

The poor people, or **peasants**, who lived on the land had to work for their lord for at least half the week. Some peasants owned small strips of land of their own. Others, called serfs, had none,

Water was too dirty and dangerous to drink so people drank milk, beer, or wine instead. Tea and coffee were drunk in the Middle East and Asia, but they had not yet been introduced into Europe.

▷ This detail from the 11th-century Bayeux Tapestry shows food being boiled in a cauldron and roasted over a spit. The sauces for the food were warmed and then taken in dishes, called saucers, to the table.

▽ The Mappa Mundi is a map of the known world in the 13th century. Like most maps drawn in the Middle Ages, it shows the world as a flat disk, surrounded by sea. People did not realize then that the world is round, not flat. The only known continents were Europe, Asia, and Africa.

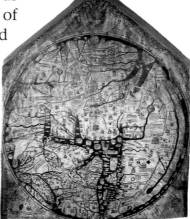

Pease pottage hot
Pease pottage cold
Pease pottage in
  a pot
Nine days old.

and worked solely for the nobles. Peasants could not leave the area controlled by the noble without permission, nor could they marry without his or her consent.

People survived on the same kinds of foods whether they lived in the north or the south of Europe. Most people ate some type of bread every day and a soupy stew called pottage, or **porridge**.

Scraps of meat or dried fish were sometimes added to the porridge, which was cooked in an iron pot, or **cauldron**, over an open wood fire. A meal of fresh fish or roast meat was a rare feast for peasants.

Many households had herb gardens. Herbs were grown mainly for medicines, but they were also used to flavor food. Honey was the sweetener for food and drinks. Sugar was almost unknown, as were foods such as turkey, potatoes, corn, and chocolate, which came to Europe from the Americas.

Fresh meat was smoked and salted to prevent it from going bad. Fish was salted, pickled, or dried. These were the only ways that people knew to keep or **preserve** food at this time. Salt and pepper were the most widely used spices for both preserving and cooking food. Venice was the great trading port for spices such as pepper and cinnamon, which **merchants** brought from Asia to Europe.

People in the countryside baked their own bread. In the towns, most people bought bread from the baker or paid for the baker to cook their own bread, pies, and meat in the baker's bread oven.

Farming and food in the countryside

Bread was the most important or **staple** food made and eaten in Europe during the Middle Ages. The grains used to make bread varied from place to place. Barley and oats were grown in the north and west, where the climate was wet and cold. Only rich people could afford to have land dug over and fertilized, or **manured**, to grow wheat, which needed good soil to grow well.

People worked in teams to farm the land. They used a large plow called a **moldboard plow.** This type of plow could clear forests and wasteland more easily and plow larger fields for crops. The moldboard was expensive to make and maintain, so people shared plows.

Farmers improved the soil by planting their crops in turn, or **rotation**, using the three-field system. The first field was planted with grain crops of wheat or rye, the second with peas,

Frumenty
(a porridge made from grains)

Take clean wheat and grind it in a **mortar**. Then fan it out and wash it clean.
Boil it until it becomes tender and brown.

△ The farm worker in this picture from the 1400s is sowing winter wheat. Grain crops were used to make porridge as well as bread and to make ale and other drinks.

▽ This illustration, drawn in 1340, shows the moldboard plow in action. Up to eight oxen were needed to pull it, and at least two people had to work the plow and drive the oxen.

Wheat made the finest white bread, but the most common bread, called *maslin*, was made from a mixture of grains. When the harvest was poor, beans, peas, and even acorns were used to make bread.

chickpeas, lentils, broad beans, oats, or barley. The third field was left unplanted, or **fallow**, for a year. The peas and beans helped to nourish the soil, so that the grain crops grew better. As more and better quality food was produced, the number of people living in Europe increased. By about A.D. 900 there were three or four times the number of people that had lived during Roman times.

However, there were many years of hunger, or **famine**, in Europe during the Middle Ages. Sometimes the crops failed or became diseased. At other times, the **plague**, or Black Death, spread across Europe and killed as many as one in three people. Then there were not enough people to work the land and produce food, so famine years followed plague years.

△ Everyone worked in the fields to harvest the grain crops. The detail from this 15th-century stained glass window shows a woman using a **sickle** to cut the crops.

"I don't have a penny," said Piers, "to buy chickens, geese or pigs. I have two fresh cheeses, a few curds and milk; an oat-cake, two loaves made of beans and bran, which I baked for my babies. By my soul, I have no salt bacon, nor an egg to cook. But I have parsley, leeks and cabbage plants to eat. We will have to live on these until, I hope, we get the harvest in."

from *Piers Plowman*, a poem written in England about 1360

▷ Bakers heated the oven by lighting a wood fire in it. Then they brushed out the embers and used wooden *peels* like these to put the small round loaves into the oven. They blocked up the entrance to keep the heat inside while the loaves were cooking.

Food and cooking in the north and south

◁ This picture, painted in the 1400s, comes from the *Book of Hours* made for the duke of Berry, the French king's brother and a great landowner in France. It shows peasants plowing the land with oxen, herding sheep, and tending the vines at the castle of Lusignan in western France.

▽ Most people in northern Europe drank ale or beer, brewed from barley, oats, or wheat. They also made cider from apples and pears. Farther south, grapes were grown to make wine. These drinks were stored in wooden barrels or casks. They were kept in locked cellars in great castles and monasteries, as theft and drunkenness were common. The only safe drink for the poorest people was **buttermilk**.

In northern Europe people relied more on livestock, mainly cattle and sheep, for food. They used milk, butter, and other dairy products in their cooking. In southern Europe, where the climate was warmer, a greater variety of crops, fresh fruit, herbs, and vegetables could be grown. Olive oil rather than butter was used for cooking.

Food was usually cooked slowly over an open wood fire. Meat was roasted on a long spike, or spit, or boiled with vegetables in a

Mutton stew

Take fair mutton that has been roasted and cut it into small pieces. Put it in a pot and add parsley, onions —minced finely— a little vinegar, wine, salt, pepper, cinnamon and saffron. If you have no wine or vinegar, use ale and mustard instead. Let it stew on the fire and then serve it forth.

from a manuscript written around 1450

▷ Some households had simple spits and a racking device to raise or lower the cauldron over the fire. Most households had shallow earthenware pans. These could be used on top of a stove, set in the open fire on a stand, or **trivet**, or left on the down hearth. A sharp knife, shaped like a dagger, and a ladle were the only other cooking utensils to be found in many homes.

△ Cats were kept in many households to kill mice and other **vermin**. This picture, drawn in Germany around 1480, shows a range of storage jars, boxes, and bottles. They were all covered to prevent vermin from spoiling the food— except for the fruit bowl!

cauldron. Some foods were baked in the ashes, or on the warm **down hearth**. Only large houses and castles had ovens, and these were often in a separate bakehouse to reduce the risk of fire to the main buildings.

People in the south used burned wood, called **charcoal** for cooking. Food could be prepared quickly, instead of roasting slowly over a fire in the heat of the summer. They also had more fresh and sun-dried fruits, herbs, and vegetables than people in the north. These foods also cooked quickly, and some could be eaten raw.

A recipe for salad

Take parsley, sage, garlic, spring onions, onions, leeks, borage, mints, fennel, cresses, rue, purslane and rosemary. Clean and wash them. Shred them into small pieces with your hands. Mix them well with oil. Put on vinegar and salt and serve it forth.

from John Russell's *Boke of Nurture*, 1393

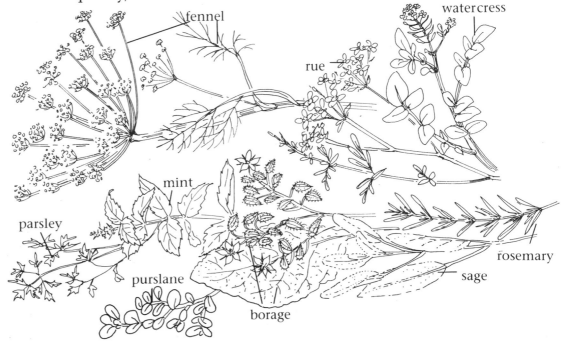

fennel

watercress

rue

mint

parsley

purslane

borage

sage

rosemary

Food through the year

▷ A 15th-century German altar cloth shows nobles eating after an autumn hunt.

The nobles enjoyed hunting deer, wild boar, and other **game**, and fishing on their lands, but the peasants were forbidden to hunt. These laws were often broken in the winter, when food stocks were low and **poaching** was almost the only way that peasants could get fresh meat and fish.

The nobles also controlled the mills and the bakehouses on their land. People had to give some of their grain in payment for using them. Women often ground their own grain and baked their own bread at home, although this, too, was forbidden. They needed all their supplies of food to survive the winter.

Sheep, goats, and cows were kept for milk and meat. There was not enough **fodder** to

△ Wildfowl were hunted with falcons. A wide variety of birds—swans, herons, thrushes, and blackbirds—was caught and eaten as well. Smaller game animals such as hares and coneys (rabbits) were often hunted, too.

Cameline sauce (a favorite sauce for game)

Soak bread in vinegar and squeeze it out. Pound ginger, cloves, cardamom, mace and plenty of cinnamon together and mix them with the bread. Salt it just right and serve it forth.

A recipe from the 1375 cookbook by Guillaume Tirel, cook to the king of France

◁ This picture of February in France was drawn about 1413. It shows a well-stocked yard, with a dovecote and beehives on the right. Outside, people are collecting firewood in the snow.

▷ This picture from *Queen Mary's Psalter*, drawn in the early 1400s, shows people knocking acorns from the trees for their pigs to eat.

feed all the animals throughout the winter. Some animals were kept for milk and breeding. Other animals were killed as food ran out.

Every rich household had a dovecote and a poultry yard. Hens were kept by everyone, but eggs were precious, so other birds and animals were fattened and killed for winter food. The only meat that peasants had to eat in the winter was bacon or pickled pork. Pigs did not need fodder in the winter months, as they could **forage** for food in the woods.

People grew potherbs (vegetables for the pot) such as onions, garlic, cabbages, and lettuce in their gardens. *Green porray* was one of the most common porridges. It was made from green vegetables and flavored with herbs.

Fish was almost as vital as bread to people in the Middle Ages. In summer, rich people ate fresh-river fish, such as salmon and trout, but for most of the year people in the countryside ate salted or dried fish, such as herring and cod.

▽ *White porray*, porridge made from leeks, was a very popular winter meal.

▽ This Flemish illustration, drawn in the 1300s, shows gut being soaked and rinsed. It was used for sausage skins.

As so much salt fish had to be eaten, many spice and herb sauces were served with it.

A green fish sauce

Take bread and soak it in vinegar, with pepper and salt. Take parsley, mint and a clove of garlic. Grind all this together, mix it with eggs and serve it forth.

from an English 15th-century cookbook

△ Most nobles had their own fishponds, called *stews*, where they bred fish such as pike and carp.

Norwegian air-dried cod or haddock, called *stockfish*, was eaten all over Europe as it was cheap and would keep for years. Stockfish was so hard that it had to be beaten with a wooden hammer, soaked, and then boiled for hours before it could be eaten.

▷ It was less work to milk one cow than ten sheep for the same amount of milk, so by the end of the Middle Ages, more dairy products were made from cow's milk.

The Church rules said that on Wednesdays, Fridays, and Saturdays no one should eat meat. In Lent, eggs and other dairy foods (called "white meats") were forbidden too. This meant that, for about half the days in the year, everyone had to eat fish.

Monasteries and large households were supplied with fresh fish from their rivers and ponds. Most other people ate preserved fish, unless they lived near the coast.

Part of a 14th-century fishmonger's stock list

"oysters, crabs, trout, sprats, porpoise, salmon, haddock, mackerel, pike, shrimps, herring, small eels, whelks, stockfish . . ."

"You will not believe how tired I am of fish and how much I wish for meat again, for I have eaten nothing but salt fish this Lent . . ."

from a 15th-century schoolbook

Millions of sheep, often in large flocks, were kept in France, Italy, Spain, and England. There was plenty of ewe's milk to drink and for making butter and cheese. Dairy products were also made from cow's milk, mainly in northern Europe, and from goat's milk in southern Europe.

Hard cheese (sometimes full of hairs or maggots) and bread were sent out to peasants working in the nobles' fields. In richer households hard cheese was grated to serve with

▽ Parsley was a favorite herb for fish sauces. Parsley juice was also used to color different foods green.

A cow became the peasant's most important possession, giving butter, cream, milk, cheese, curds, and whey.

▷ Beekeeping methods have hardly changed since this picture was painted.

△ Milk being churned in a wooden barrel to make butter.

During Lent, rich households used *almond milk* made of wine, ground almonds, and honey as a substitute for real milk, which was forbidden.

Rissoles for Lent

Take figs and boil them in ale. When they are tender pound the figs into small pieces in a mortar. Take pears and dates and shred them in with the figs. Soak the dried fish until it is soft and then shred it into the mixture. Shape the mixture into balls. Flour them and dip them in batter. Then cook them in oil and serve forth.

from an English cookbook, written in the 15th century

macrows (macaroni and cheese), or mixed with herbs and eggs to make *herbolace* (a dish between scrambled eggs and an omelet). Every household had its own special selection of fresh herbs to mix with soft curd cheese to make *spermyse*.

Eggs with *collops* (strips of bacon or salted pork), a piece of bread smeared with butter or oil, and buttermilk might be the main meal of the day in poorer households. According to a 14th-century book, a summer treat was "raw cream eaten with strawberries or bilberries."

Eggs were widely used in richer households for dishes such as custards. They were made from egg yolks and cream, sweetened with honey, yellowed with saffron, and decorated with violet or borage flowers. Egg yolks, honey, wine, and bread crumbs were gently heated to make *caudles* to drink at breakfast or at bedtime.

◁ The woman who is feeding the chickens has been spinning wool. She holds a spinning staff under her arm. The drawing comes from the *Luttrell Psalter*, made around 1340.

Food in towns and cities

△ Pottery jugs were used to carry and serve drinks such as wine, ale, and water. Only very poor people drank water.

▽ This detail, from a 13th-century stained glass window in Chartres Cathedral, France, shows fishmongers at work.

◁ French shops and market stalls in the 1400s. The spice stall on the right also sells sugar, grated from the large white cone or sugarloaf. Merchants bought so many spices, particularly pepper, in bulk, *en gros* in French, that the spice traders became known as grocers.

People who lived in the towns relied on food brought in from the surrounding countryside by farmers and traders. They also had the opportunity to buy a greater variety of **imported** foods, spices, and drinks from the merchants who were based in the larger towns and cities.

There were strict rules governing how food was sold in most towns and cities. These rules related to the quality and price of food and drink and to the people who sold them. They also stated how and where foods such as meat and fish were to be prepared and sold. Many of these rules were ignored.

In 1345 a law was passed in London forbidding "Folks from bringing poultry to the City and selling it in lanes, houses and elsewhere in secret."

During the early 1400s the king of France commanded "that the air be not infected by the smell of slaughterhouses and that the water of the River Seine be not polluted with the blood and filth of dead animals. All slaughterhouses shall be established outside the city of Paris."

A famous London cookshop

Depending on the time of year you may find meats—roast, fried and boiled, birds and fish both great and small. Some dishes are for poorer people, the more delicate—such as venison—are for the rich. If friends, weary with travel, should suddenly arrive and are too hungry to wait for fresh food to be bought and cooked for them, they hurry to the river bank. There they will find everything they might wish, ready for them to eat.

from a description by William Fitz-Stephen, written before 1183

△ Tripe being prepared, cooked, and eaten at a tavern in Lombardy, Italy, in the late 14th century.

▷ A drawing of a butcher at work in Germany in the late 14th century. The animal was hung at the back of the shop until it was cut up and weighed, ready for sale.

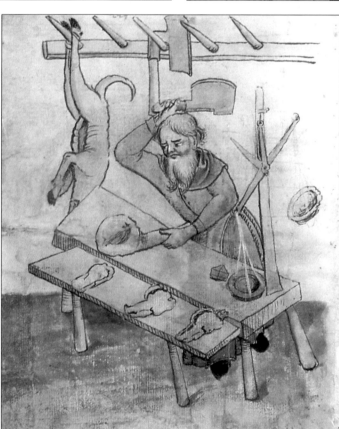

The 90,000 people who lived in the Italian city of Florence in the 14th century ate 4,000 oxen and calves, 60,000 sheep, 20,000 goats, and 30,000 pigs every year.

During the 12th century in Paris, a pig ran between the legs of a horse. The rider—a prince—fell and fractured his skull. The king then passed a law forbidding the rearing of pigs in French towns and cities.

A law was passed in 1481 in Frankfurt, forbidding pigsties on the streets in front of people's houses.

Fresh food and snacks were sold on the streets and in the markets. Cookshops provided hot food for take-out, while inns or **taverns** served drinks and prepared hot meals for their customers.

Most town households had small gardens or yards, where people kept animals such as hens and pigs, so there were also rules to prevent animals from roaming through the streets.

△ These drawings from the *Luttrell Psalter* show food for a feast being prepared.

Food for the nobles

Rulers held meetings at **court** with their nobles and advisers—the courtiers—and with Church leaders, bishops, and archbishops. They made laws for the towns as well as for the country-side that they controlled. Anyone who wanted to influence the decisions made by the rulers, such as merchants and traders who might want a law changed in their favor, had to attend the court to do so.

Large numbers of servants, from clerks to

▽ On the left of this picture from the *Luttrell Psalter* the cooked food is being cut up and put on serving dishes. The sauces for the different dishes are being made at the table in the middle of the picture. On the right, servants are taking the food to the dining hall.

△ The next course of food arrives from the kitchen.

In France a law stated that bishops touring the countryside should have a daily supply of 50 loaves, 50 eggs, 10 chickens, and 5 pigs provided for them.

stable hands, were needed by the courtiers and visitors to the court. Some servants were part of the ruler's household, while others worked for the nobles or merchants.

When rulers toured the countryside with their court, or Church leaders visited monasteries, there were rules about who should provide food and lodging for them all.

The kitchen of a large house, monastery, or castle had stone floors and walls with great wide fireplaces where most of the cooking was done. The bakehouse and dairy were usually in separate buildings. There were storerooms between the kitchen and the dining hall, and a pantry from which bread and salt were served.

There were only two large pieces of furniture in the kitchen. A heavy table was used as a work surface, where vegetables were cut up, and there was a chopping block for meat joints.

Meat was roasted on spits or grilled, using a grid of metal bars on a long handle that was set over the fire. Other food was boiled in cauldrons hooked onto pothangers over the fire. Other long-handled metal pots and pans were held over the fire for making sauces or boiling eggs.

▽ This 12th-century German drawing shows a king and queen being served.

◁ The tables were laid with cloths, knives, salt cellars, trenchers, and rolls before the food was served.

Medieval feasts

The medieval banquet, or feast, provided food for everyone, not only the rich and powerful. Rules were laid down for every aspect of such a feast, including the way that food was prepared and served, where people sat and what they ate, their behavior, and table manners.

▽ Only the most important people were served individually. Everyone else ate in pairs or fours. Each set of two or four people was known as a *cover*.

Some table manners

He should not laugh, speak or sing with his mouth full and should eat without much noise.

He should not lean on his elbows at the table nor dip his fingers into his drink.

He should not dip his fingers too deep in a shared dish, nor crumble bread into it.

He should clean his spoon properly, not leave it in the dish. Neither must he pick his teeth with his knife, blow on his food to cool it, or wipe his mouth on the table cloth. He should not gnaw bones nor tear meat to bits with his fingers.

◁ All the food and drink served to the nobles was tasted first, to ensure that it was not poisoned or going bad. The *sewer*, or head waiter, tasted the food, while the cupbearer tasted the drink.

▽ French hunters being served lunch in the late 14th century

The host, and the most important guests and family, sat at a table on a raised platform at one end of the hall. The table nearest them on the right of the host was called the *rewarde*, because it was served with dishes from the host's table. Other tables were arranged according to the importance of the people sitting at them and were served with different foods accordingly.

At least three main courses were served at a feast. Guests could choose from a variety of dishes, including sweet ones, for every course. Each different kind of meat or fish was served with its own special sauce.

Roast meats were served first, before the fish. The carver placed the best pieces of meat on the important guests' trenchers. The rest was carved and put on large plates or platters at the table. Other foods came straight from the kitchen in dishes for two or four people to share.

Trenchers were not eaten but collected in baskets after the feast and given to the poor.

◁ Craftworkers, such as jewelers and dressmakers and musicians and other entertainers came to the court. They provided goods, services, and entertainment for the nobles at banquets and feasts.

▽ "When he [the peacock] is roasted, let him cool. Then wind the skin with the feathers and the tail about the body and serve him forth as if he were alive."

The table at a medieval feast was full of color and decoration. Many foods were not only highly spiced and scented, but also brightly colored. Jellies and custards were multicolored, with red, yellow, green, or purple dyes from plants. Other foods, such as meatballs, were coated with real gold for very special feasts. Swans and peacocks were stuffed (sometimes with other cooked birds inside them) and put on the table complete with their feathers.

The mixture of sweet and spicy dishes served at each course included dishes called *soteltes*. These were sweets, jellies, and pastries made and molded into different shapes, such as crowns. Some were made to look as though they were life-size wild animals, such as eagles and lions. Although the *soteltes* could be eaten, they were mainly for decoration.

Guests were not expected to eat every dish that was served for each course at a feast, but to choose from the dishes they were offered.

Sometimes swans were served with gold-coated feathers and a crown or garland on their heads. A vinegary hot sauce called *chaudron* was made to go with swan meat.

◁ Some dishes such as venison and sturgeon were served only to the nobles. Monks and priests were forbidden meat, except for game. Musicians entertained the guests while each course was cleared away and the next served. Leftover food was given to the poor.

This was the menu for a French royal wedding banquet in 1403.

First meat course

Head of wild boar, armed with tusks and decorated, served with a hot spicy gravy and a pudding of rice, spices, wine, and honey
Cygnets, chickens, pheasants, herons
Puddings
A *sotelte*

First fish course

Soup, salty fish, spiced lampreys
Pike, bream, roast salmon
Fish pies
Fritters
A *sotelte*

Second meat course

Venison cooked with frumenty and served with a jelly
Stuffed piglets
Rabbits, bitterns, stuffed chicken, partridge
Bread and dried fruits, sliced and fried
A *sotelte*

Second fish course

Porpoise with frumenty and a jelly
Bream, salmon, eels, lampreys in batter, plaice
Bread and dried fruits, sliced and fried
A *sotelte* in the shape of a crowned panther

Third meat course

Cream of almonds, pears in syrup
Venison roasted
Woodcock, plover, rabbits, quails, fieldfare pies
A *sotelte*

Third fish course

Cream of almonds, pears in syrup
Grilled tench, trout, fried flounders, perch
Roast lampreys, sturgeon, crabs, and shrimps
A *sotelte* in the shape of a crowned eagle

Food for travelers

Most people who worked the land for the nobles were forbidden to travel far. Some of them probably walked to the nearest market to sell their produce or to buy livestock. The food they ate on these journeys was simple— perhaps a piece of bread and some hard cheese. When nobles raised armies for their rulers, some of the peasants became foot soldiers. Soldiers lived off the land, taking livestock and supplies of food as they traveled to war. Many areas of farmland in Europe were ruined by armies during the frequent wars of the Middle Ages.

Monasteries provided food and lodging for **pilgrims** and other travelers. In some monasteries the monks dined as well as the nobles. In other religious houses there were strict rules, so

Scottish soldiers carried a metal bakestone and a bag of oatmeal which they used to "make a thin cake like a biscuit, which they eat to warm their stomachs. It is no wonder that they perform a longer day's march than other soldiers."

from *Chronicles* by Sir Jean Froissart, written during the wars in Britain in the early 14th century

▷ The main trading towns and cities in the Middle Ages were on the coasts, where there were good harbors, and inland on river crossing points or where trading routes met.

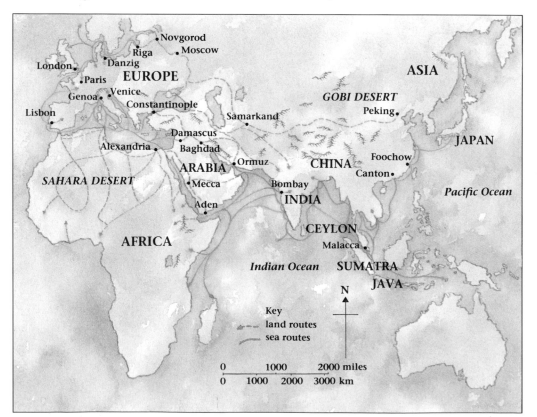

Novgorod
Riga
Moscow
London
Danzig
Paris
EUROPE
ASIA
Venice
Genoa
GOBI DESERT
Constantinople
Lisbon
Peking
Samarkand
JAPAN
Damascus
Alexandria
Baghdad
Foochow
Ormuz
CHINA
Canton
ARABIA
Mecca
Bombay
Aden
INDIA
Pacific Ocean
SAHARA DESERT
CEYLON
AFRICA
Malacca
Indian Ocean
SUMATRA
JAVA
N

Key
land routes
sea routes

0   1000   2000 miles
0   1000   2000   3000 km

◁ This view of Venice was drawn in 1338. The buildings were richly decorated with materials from the East. Travelers and merchants waited by the waterways and harbors for their ships to come in.

the monks ate simple food, like the ordinary people in the countryside around them.

Traders rode from one market to another, carrying their goods, such as cloth, pepper-corns, salt, and other spices, on packhorses, donkeys, or mules. They ate and sometimes stayed at the taverns in the towns. They brought news and travelers' tales of faraway places, including descriptions of different foods and fashions for cooking with the spices they sold.

Merchants traveled all over Europe by land and sea. Some went to western France, the Netherlands, and Scotland to buy salt. Others brought ale, wool, and cloth from England and the Netherlands or fish and furs from northern Europe. Many merchants traded in wine from Germany, Spain, and France. Venice, in Italy, was the center for the most important trade between Europe and Asia in silk and spices.

▷ Women brewed ale or beer in many households, and some ran alehouses for travelers. A long pole with a *bush* (usually a bunch of ivy) at the end of it was hung above the door to show that ale or beer was for sale.

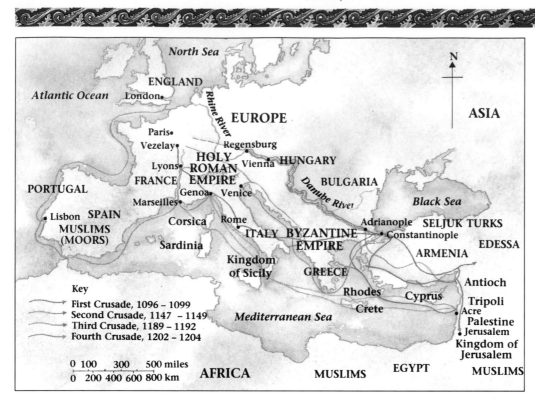

North Sea

ENGLAND

Atlantic Ocean London•

Rhine River

EUROPE

N

ASIA

Paris•
Vezelay•   Regensburg
            HOLY   Vienna HUNGARY
    Lyons• ROMAN
FRANCE EMPIRE   BULGARIA
PORTUGAL   Genoa• Venice   Danube River
                                        Black Sea
    •Lisbon SPAIN Corsica Rome
MUSLIMS   ITALY BYZANTINE   Adrianople SELJUK TURKS
(MOORS)   Sardinia   EMPIRE   •Constantinople   EDESSA
                        Kingdom   ARMENIA
    Marseilles•   of Sicily GREECE   Antioch
Key   Rhodes   Cyprus   Tripoli
First Crusade, 1096 – 1099   Crete   Acre
Second Crusade, 1147 – 1149 Mediterranean Sea   Palestine
Third Crusade, 1189 – 1192   •Jerusalem
Fourth Crusade, 1202 – 1204   Kingdom of
0 100   300   500 miles   Jerusalem
0 200 400 600 800 km AFRICA   MUSLIMS   EGYPT   MUSLIMS

◁ The map shows the routes of the first four Crusades. Nobles and soldiers from all over Europe set out on these long journeys to the Middle East. Monks, priests, and even children traveled on some of the Crusades.

In Siena, Italy, **nuns** first made *panforte* for the Crusaders. The rich, spicy, sweet mixture with nuts and dried fruit was pressed into a round, flat shape. It was easy to carry and it kept well. More than 30 different types of panforte are on sale in Siena today.

▽ This picture, painted around 1237 in Baghdad, shows a trader about to mount his camel. Arab merchants controlled the trade routes through Muslim lands from Europe to the East. They used donkeys, camels, or mules, roped together in long lines called caravans, to carry their goods.

For more than 200 years Christian armies from Europe fought a series of wars called Crusades. They were trying to recapture the land where Jesus was born, including the city of Jerusalem, from the Muslim peoples who ruled it. The first of the Crusades, in 1096, was the most successful for the Christian armies. Later, the Muslim armies regained control of their lands and further Crusades took place, without success for the Christians.

Sometimes trading ships and fishing boats were at sea for months at a time. Some ships carried passengers—travelers and Crusaders—as well as spices and other goods for trade.

The ships also carried supplies of grain, salt pork, beef and bacon, salt fish, hard cheese, vinegar, and ale for the crew. The food supplies usually got wet and went bad. Sailors often waited until it was dark before eating their food, so that they couldn't see the maggots in it!

Some travelers, such as Marco Polo and Friar Odoric, followed the trading routes from

Fishermen carried up to a ton of salt on their boats so that they could preserve their catch on board. They salted the fish and packed them into wooden barrels.

Ship's biscuit was made of a flour and water dough that was baked and dried until it was rock hard. It could be kept for 50 years. Sailors soaked it until it broke up like porridge and ate it with salt pork or fish and a dash of vinegar.

◁ Friar Odoric, a monk from Udine in Italy, was sent to Asia in 1316 as a missionary. He traveled from Persia to India and then to China. He spent three years there before returning overland to Italy, probably through Tibet. He wrote an account of his travels that was very popular and well known in Europe.

Europe overland through Asia to China. They described the different foods they saw and ate on their travels. The Italians, in particular, used these descriptions and the spices that merchants brought back from the East to produce a wide variety of dishes. Their cooking was famous throughout the courts of Europe. However, the food for ordinary people was unchanged for hundreds of years.

◁ Marco Polo, a merchant from Venice, traveled through Asia to China. He stayed there for 17 years, working for the emperor Kublai Khan. The picture shows the emperor's birthday feast. Marco Polo returned to Venice in 1295. The account of his travels, *Il milione*, was an immediate success in Italy and his stories were told all over Europe.

Medieval Meals

Some of the dishes eaten in the Middle Ages are still popular today. These menus can help you plan simple meals or a medieval feast. The ingredients are similar but the taste may be different from dishes served in medieval times.

The ways we preserve foods today, by canning and freezing, had not yet been invented. The taste of foods preserved by drying, salting, and pickling is different from those that are canned or frozen.

The range of fruits and vegetables used in medieval cooking is much smaller than today. Tomatoes and potatoes from the Americas and tropical fruits such as bananas were unknown.

Medieval cooks had to use food produced locally. There were no planes, trucks, or trains to transport food quickly from one part of the world to another. The choice of fresh fruit, vegetables, and herbs depended on what was growing in local gardens during a particular season. In the winter there was less fresh food. Cooks had to use more preserved foods—salted meats, pickled or smoked fish, and dried vegetables.

Breakfast
Peasant style

Rye *or* whole meal bread
with Cheddar cheese
Buttermilk

Breakfast
Noble style

White *or* whole meal rolls
with butter
Smoked herring *or* kippers
Pickled herrings
Whole milk

Lunch
Peasant style

Rye *or* whole meal bread

Cheddar cheese
or
Bacon and eggs
Buttermilk

Lunch
Noble style

Toast with honey

Gingerbread

Cinnamon biscuits *or* cakes

Warmed milk with honey
or
Warmed grape juice with cloves and cinnamon

Dinner
Peasant style

These dishes would be served with rye
or whole meal bread

Thick leek soup
served with fresh chopped parsley
or
Baked beans topped with fried chopped bacon
pieces
or
Pease porridge—a thick paste of mashed peas,
with lots of salt and pepper

Wine *or* ale *or* buttermilk

(Serve grape juice *or* ginger ale
instead of wine *or* ale)

Dinner
Noble style

First course
Boiled cod with parsley sauce

Spit-roast *or* barbecued chicken stuffed with
grapes *or* onions

Beef *or* mutton olives

Apple fritters

Second course
Trout coated with bread crumbs and fried in
butter with almonds

Roast beef with garlic sauce

Chicken pasties *or* pies

A meat tile—four dishes:
Sautéed pieces of chicken *or* veal; Crayfish tails;
Toasted bread with almonds; Stewed lamb

Pears cooked with cloves and cinnamon in honey

Third course
Roast venison

Blancmange—rice cooked with minced pieces
of chicken, ground almonds, and milk

Green salad with herbs

Fish *or* eel pasties

Dairioles—small custard tarts with mace,
cinnamon, and minced dates sprinkled on top

Wines and ale
(Serve grape juice *or* ginger ale
instead of wine *or* ale)

Recipes

Here are some recipes for medieval dishes that you, your family, and friends could eat today. Ask an adult for help when you plan the meals and start to prepare the food.

> **WARNING:** Sharp knives and boiling liquids are dangerous. Hot ovens and pans can burn you. *Always ask an adult to help you* when you are preparing or cooking food in the kitchen.

Thick leek soup

Ingredients

1 lb fresh leeks

1 cup dried mixed vegetables (pearl barley, yellow split peas, lentils)

$1/2$ cup butter

$1^1/_2$ pints milk

salt and pepper

3 T fresh chopped parsley

1. Put the mixed dried vegetables into a mixing bowl and cover them with cold water. Let them soak overnight.
2. Drain and rinse the vegetables.
3. Wash and clean the leeks thoroughly. Carefully chop them into small rings, taking care to keep your fingers away from the blade of the knife.
4. Melt the butter in the saucepan over a low heat and stir in the leeks.
5. Mix the soaked vegetables with the leeks and butter. Then pour in the milk.
6. Stir in the salt and pepper and cook the soup slowly over a low heat. Do not let the milk boil.
7. Cook the vegetables until they are soft, about one to one-and-a-half hours. Take the saucepan off the heat.
8. Carefully chop the parsley very fine.
9. Pour the soup into a serving dish or bowls and sprinkle the parsley over the top.

Equipment

large mixing bowl

colander

cutting board

sharp knife

measuring cup

large saucepan

wooden spoon

serving dish or bowls

Ask an adult to help you when you start to cook.

Hot liquids and sharp knives are dangerous.

"Pease porridge"

Ingredients

$1^1/_4$ cups dried green peas

2 cups milk

$1/2$ tsp salt

$1/2$ tsp black pepper

1. Put the dried peas into a mixing bowl and cover them with cold water. Let them soak overnight.
2. Drain and rinse the peas.
3. Put the peas in a saucepan with the milk and cook them slowly over a low heat. Do not let the

Equipment

large mixing bowl

colander

measuring cup

large saucepan

potato masher

wooden spoon

serving dish

milk boil.

4. Stir the peas occasionally so that they don't stick to the pan.
5. When the peas are soft, (about about one to one-and-a-half hours) take the saucepan off the heat and mash the peas into a smooth paste.
6. Stir in the black pepper and salt.
7. Put the mixture into a serving dish.

Ask an adult to help you when you start to cook.
Hot liquids and pans are dangerous.

Lamb stew

Ingredients
1 lb cold roast lamb
2 tsp chopped parsley
1 medium onion, finely chopped
1 cinnamon stick
salt and pepper
pinch of saffron
2 tsp red wine vinegar
7 fl oz red grape juice
4 tsp honey

1. Carefully chop the meat into small pieces and put them in a saucepan.
2. Carefully chop the onion and the parsley very fine.
3. Add the parsley, onion, and cinnamon stick to the meat and season with salt and pepper.
4. Scatter the saffron over the meat and then pour the wine vinegar and grape juice over it.
5. Bring the liquid to a boil and then turn the heat down. Let the mixture cook slowly until the onion is soft and the meat warmed through, about half an hour.
6. Add honey until the juice is like syrup.
7. Pour the stew into a serving dish.

Equipment
cutting board
sharp knife
measuring cup
large saucepan
serving dish

Ask an adult to help you when you start to cook.
Sharp knives and boiling liquids are dangerous.

"Pokerounce"
Honey toast with pine nuts

Ingredients
1 cup clear honey
a pinch of ground ginger
a pinch of cinnamon
a pinch of ground black pepper
4 large slices of white bread
1 T pine nuts

1. Put the honey, spices, and pepper in a small saucepan on a very low heat, until the honey thins. Do not let the honey boil or burn.
2. Let the mixture cool.
3. Toast the bread lightly on both sides.
4. Cut each slice into four small squares.
5. Put the slices onto plates or a serving dish.
6. Pour the honey mixture over the toast.
7. Stick the pine nuts upright into each piece of toast so they look like small stakes.

Equipment
measuring cup
small saucepan
knife
serving dish or plates

Ask an adult to help you when you start to cook.
Hot liquids and pans are dangerous.

Glossary

buttermilk: The sour liquid left when the butter has been separated from the milk, after churning.

cauldron: A large pot, usually made of iron, for boiling water and cooking over an open fire.

charcoal: Small pieces of burned wood used for fuel.

court: The place where people who advised the king or ruler met. It was also the name given to the people who made up the court.

down hearth: The part of the hearth farthest from the fire, used for cooking or warming foods gently.

fallow: Land that has usually been plowed, but not planted with crops. Land was normally left fallow for a year, to recover after planting.

famine: A time when there was not enough food and people starved.

feudal system: The way in which land and property were owned and worked during the Middle Ages.

fodder: Food for animals. Hay and straw were sometimes stored for winter fodder.

forage: To wander freely, looking for food.

game: Animals, birds, and fish that are hunted for food or sport.

import: Goods brought into one country from another.

manor: The area of land and property given to a noble by the ruler.

manure: Animal waste spread on the land to enrich the soil.

merchants: People who bought and sold goods, often from other countries.

moldboard plow: A plow, made of wood, with three working parts. The knife blade or *coulter* at the front went straight into the ground, the plowshare behind it cut through shallow grass roots horizontally, and two blades and a shaped board—the moldboard—at the back turned the turf over to the side.

monastery: The buildings and land where monks live and work together.

mortar: A strong bowl or dish in which foods were ground into small pieces or powder, using a club or stick called a *pestle*.

nun: A woman who has devoted her life to God, and usually lives and works with a community of nuns in a convent.

peasants: Poor people who worked on the land.

pilgrim: Someone who travels to visit a special holy place.

plague: A disease carried by fleas and spread by black rats. There was no known cure during the Middle Ages.

poaching: Taking or killing animals, birds, or fish without permission on someone else's land.

porridge: A soup or stew, thickened with vegetables, legumes, or grains until it is almost solid. Meat or fish might be added, or milk and honey to sweeten it.

preserve: To treat food or drink so that it could be kept for a long time without going bad. The main ways of preserving food in the Middle Ages were salting, drying, pickling, and smoking. Salt, pepper, vinegar, and oil were commonly used to help preserve food. Frozen and canned foods were unknown at this time.

rotation: The usual order for crop rotation was a grain crop, then a bean or pulse crop, then no crop at all for a year.

sickle: A tool with a curved blade and a short handle, used for cutting back undergrowth and harvesting crops.

spit: A long thin metal bar, often pointed at one end, on which food is fixed to be cooked.

staple: The most important food, crop, or goods produced in any area.

sweetmeats: Sweet candied fruits, small spicy cakes, marzipan, and nougat.

tavern: A place where ale, beer, and wine are sold and drunk. In the Middle Ages taverns often served hot meals as well.

trivet: A three-legged stand for a pot, usually made of iron.

vermin: Small animals and insects that can harm animals and food, or plants and crops.

Further reading

Aliki. *A Medieval Feast*. New York: HarperCollins Children's Books, 1981.

Caselli, Giovanni. *The Middle Ages*. New York: Peter Bedrick Books, 1988.

Corbishley, Mike. *Middle Ages*. New York: Facts on File, 1990.

Cosman, Madeleine Pelsner. *Medieval Holidays and Festivals*. New York: Scribner's, 1981.

Howarth, Sarah. *Medieval People*. Brookfield, Conn.: Millbrook Press, 1992.

———. *Medieval Places*. Brookfield, Conn.: Millbrook Press, 1992.

Oakes, Catherine. *The Middle Ages*. San Diego: Harcourt Brace, 1989.

Index